SOUN OF WORDS

Book 2

T. Muir

HODDER
GIBSON
PART OF HACHETTE LIVRE UK

INTRODUCTION

This book aims at providing a sure phonic basis for the child who cannot read. It is therefore of use to non-readers of all ages, especially those in Tutorial Groups. It is not a Reading Book, but it is meant to be used in conjunction with any one of the many excellent books on the market that provide material for "Look and Say" and "Sentence" Methods but little or none for phonic work. An activity book entitled Sound and Write — Book 2 is also available to reinforce the phonic skills taught in this book.

Before starting this book teachers might be interested in reading on the last page methods and techniques used by the authoress as a result of her considerable experience.

HOW TO USE THIS BOOK

1. Use the pictures for Oral Composition.
2. Use the words and pictures in your Speech Training Lessons.
3. Let the book save your time by allowing it to take the place of the many cards you have in the past so laboriously made by hand.
4. Let it help you towards a rapid assessment of the reading level of any new pupil.
5. Use it for quick revisal with any child whose reading is patchy.
6. If you work on individual or group plans, you will find here a means of employing fruitfully any child on whom you are not focussing your immediate attention. You can do this:
    (a) By providing young children with a board and coloured chalks (to copy pictures) and white chalk (to copy words).
    (b) By providing other children with coloured pencils, ordinary pencil and a cheap jotter.
    (c) By having word lists copied, as individual writing lessons.
7. Allow older children to illustrate words chosen by themselves from lists.
8. Select words for Spelling Lessons from the lists, teaching the words in "families", graded according to difficulty. Do not start actual spelling until phonic basis is very firmly established.
9. Before starting this book, teachers might be interested in reading on the last page methods and techniques used by the authoress as a result of her considerable experience.

<u>Revisal</u>

wh	sh	ng	ch	th
	king	when	shop	
	this	wing	chips	
	along	whip	church	
	then	ding-dong	sit	
	sitting	hop	hopping	
	fish	fishing	shop	
	shopping	chat	chatting	
	think	thinking		

sh	wh	ch	ng	th

There must be instant recognition of sh, wh, ch, ng, th.

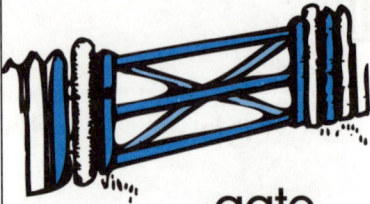

gate

rake

cake

hare

safe

cradle

name

whale

table

tape

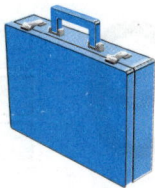

a—e

case	case
ca—e	cake
da—e	care
ga—e	came
ha—e	wave
la—e	wake
ma—e	made
na—e	date
sa—e	late
ba—e	bathe

Teach rule that silent "e" (giving name), makes "a" say ā. Starters now read as if they were written cay, day, gay, hay, lay, etc.

pie

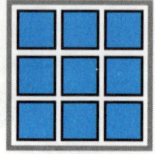

nine

pipe

fire

hive

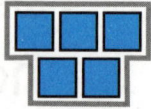

five

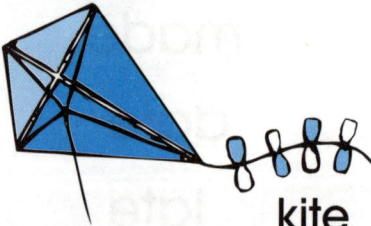

kite

fire-side

tiles

lines

i—e

	wire	pipe
tie	wipe	ride
lie	wide	chime
die	hide	white
wi—e	nine	shine
hi—e	side	prize
di—e	time	fire
bi—e	tide	like
si—e	mile	hive
ri—e	mine	tire

State the rule: Silent "e" makes "i" say ī. Be sure to practise starters.

7

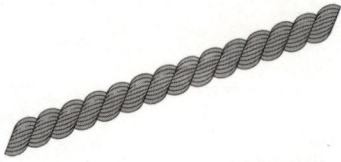

rope

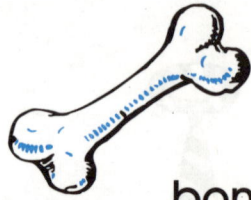

bone

cone

rose

nose

mole

smoke

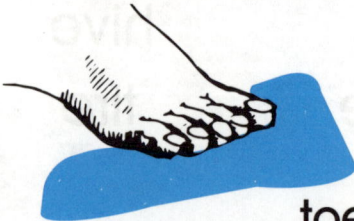

toes

sole

o—e

	hole	rose
toes	home	choke
foe	stone	sore
woe	joke	pole
doe	nose	shore
bo—e	bone	those
ho—e	vote	broke
so—e	doze	store
jo—e	woke	stole
no—e	wore	clothes

State the rule

tube	here
tune	Peter
cube	see
cure	wee
use	bee
rude	me
pure	he
glue	we
blue	she
true	fever

State these rules.

fly	tie	blind
sky	die	find
try	died	mind
dry	cried	kind
fry	fried	hind
cry	tried	child
shy	spied	wild
by	shied	mild
my		

<u>Revisal</u>

bare, bite, bone, tube, pure,
lecture, five, glue, goes,
able, table, stable, cable,
die, died, cry, cried, sly.

---

hope	shine	choke
hoping	shining	choking
ride	wave	care
riding	waving	caring

Revisal

taste, paste, waste, pastry, dive, diver, enjoy, even, evening, fire-side, figure, idle, ladle, lame, lady, ladies, length, join, mole, mar'ma'lade, morning, safe, noise, noisy, oil, piper, plate, point, pointer, poison, prize, punch, size, skates, skating, boxing, sliding, ashes, alone, bathe, bathing, brave, file, capture, these, those, tiger, wife, wise, yelling, boiling.

tray

haystack

pray

crayons

sail

chain

chair

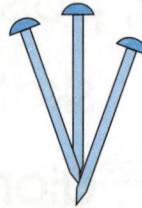
nails

mail-box

stair

ay   ai

tray	fai´	fai´l
may	hai´	hai´r
say	lai´	lai´d
day	mai´	pai´l
way	rai´	rai´n
away	sai´	sai´l
hay	pai´	mai´d
pay	jai´	jai´l
ray	sai´l	nai´ls
play	sai´ling	afrai´d

State the rule: "ay" (saying names) sounds ā. Also "ai" sounds ā.

 wheel

 tree

 bee

 reel

 sheep

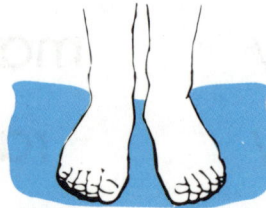 feet

 beech-nut

 see-saw

 bo-peep

3  three

e e

	see	wee
tree	cree'p	week
fee't	shee't	sweep
fee'l	flee't	sweet
see'd	bree'ze	thir,teen
see'n	stee'r	fif,teen
bee'f	bee'n	six,teen
dee'p	fee'd	seven,teen
pee'p	mee't	nine,teen
stee'l	see'm	cheers

State each new rule as you elicit it.

 **beads**

 **steam**

 **bean**

 **sheaf**

 **sea**

 **ear**

 **seat**

 **tea-pot**

 **leaves**

 **seal**

e a

	ear	shears
bea'ds	eat	reach
rea'd	seat	team
mea'n	leak	cream
bea'n	cheat	dream
lea'f	wheat	tea
lea'd	clear	sea
dea'r	leash	pea
hea'r	teach	spear
hea'p	teacher	speak

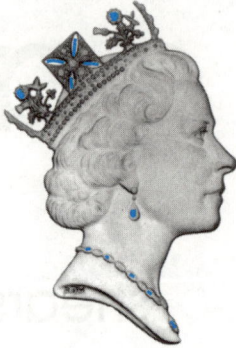

queen	squirrel
quick	squeak
quilt	squeal
quack	squint
quite	squibs
quarter	square
question	squid

Quack, quack, quack

qu = kw

sh,   ng,   wh,   th,   ch,   qu,

ay, ai,   ee, ea,   ie,

a — e,   e — e,   i — e,

o — e,   u — e,   ng,   oe,

ch,   ay,   wh,   ee,

sh,   ea,   th,   ai,   ie,

qu,   sh,   ay,   qu,

ay,   ai,   ee,   ea,

th,   qu,   ch,   ng,   wh.

There must be immediate recognition of these letter combinations.

 boots

 book

 scooter

 roof

 stool

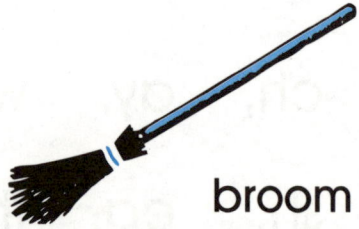 broom

 moon

 roots

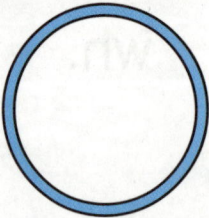 hoop

 spoon

o o

	too	took
boo'k	boo'k	stool
loo'	loo'k	brook
roo'	roo'm	crook
moo'	moo'n	spoon
coo'	coo'k	shook
soo'	soo't	tooth
hoo'	hoo'k	poor
foo'	foo'd	pool
zoo'	zoo'm	stool

 cow

 crown

 clown

 tower

 flower

 brownie

 house

 mouse

 spout

 trout

ow

ou

ow	ou
cow	trou'sers
now	ou'r
how	flou'r
bow	cou'nt
dow'n	cou'ch
tow'n	fou'nd
drow'n	rou'nd
brow'n	sou'nd
	ou't
tow'er	shou't
show'er	a,bou't
flow'er	sou'th
crow'd	pou'nd
row'ans	pou'ch
bow'-wow	

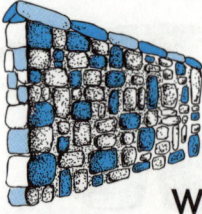 wall

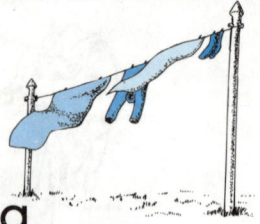 washing

 swan

 swallow

 dwarf

 wand

 watch

 wasp

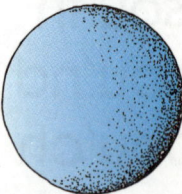 ball

 stall

 **w a**   **a w**

wa'll	s aw
wa'sh	j aw
wa'shing	r aw
wa'nt	p aw
wa'r	dr aw
wa's	
wa'sp	
wa'tch	
wa'nd	
wa'lk	**all**
wa'rm	
wa'rt	
wa'ter	b all
swa'n	c all
swa'llow	t all
dwa'rf	f all

Teach that "a" with "ll" says "aw".

27

 coal

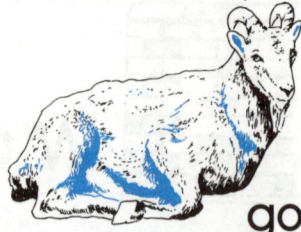 goat

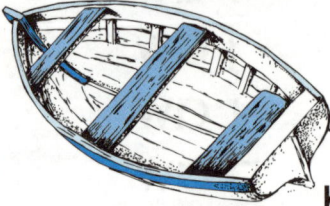 boat

 road

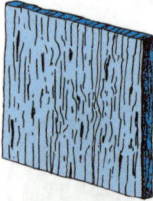 board

 toad

 coat

 oak-leaf

 loaf

 soap

o a

roa'	
soa'	
boa'	loaf
coa'	load
foa'	road
moa'	roast
toa'	roar
cloa'	goal
cloa'k	goat
soa'k	toad
soa'p	loan
coa'ch	toast
coa't	float
boa't	oak
coa'l	oars
foa'l	oats
foa'm	oat-meal

 crow

 arrow

 barrow

 window

 bowl

 throw

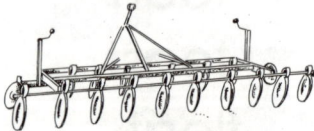 harrow

 lawn-mower

 bow

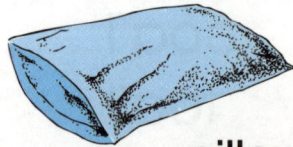 pillow

O W

crow
low
blow
slow
row
mow
mow'er
mow'ing
sow
sow'ing
grow
grow'ing
bow
snow
show
shown

low
below
arrow
barrow
harrow
sparrow
swallow
pillow
fellow
bellow
yellow
shallow

throw
elbow
shadow
window
Glasgow
widow

 mice

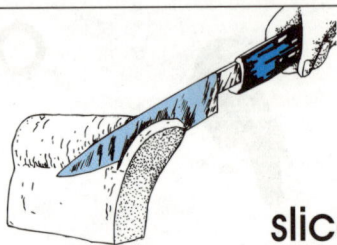 slice

 ice

 dice

 ace

 race

 face

 lace

 bicycle

 tricycle

ce = s

dice	ace
ice	lace
mice	race
rice	space
nice	face
price	
twice	prince
thrice	princess
slice	dance
cell	concert
cellar	voice

ce, oe, ao, ow, oo, wa,
ou, ow, all, aw, ce, ie,
ng, sh, th, ch, wh, qu, oe,
a—e, e—e, i—e, o—e, u—e.

33

cage

orange

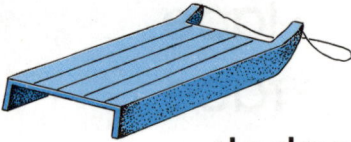
sledge

bridge

ge = j

cage	edge
age	hedge
rage	sledge
page	bridge
wages	midges
stage	hinge
budgie	ginger
lodger	pigeon

Easy words for revision

in, at, up, is, ill, for, his, man, hen, pick, box, cut, clock, pram, went, will, blunt, Molly, Fanny, Jimmy, Jackie, Jenny, ink, sink, donkey, little, ship, with, chop, where, sing, came, here, like, bone, tune, my, see, day, hair, me, she, eat, quick, book, cow, our, was, road, low, all, call, ice, mice, saw, paws, ace, race, bridge, stage.

knife	knob
knot	knee

"k" before "n" is silent

knot	know
knob	known
knit	knelt
knitting	knocking
knock	knife
knocker	knives
knocked	knap-sack
knee	
knees	
kneel	

wreath

wreck

wren

abcdefghij
write well
writing

"w" before "r" is silent

wrong	1. one
wrap	2. two
write	3. three
writing	4. four
writer	5. five
wreck	6. six
wrist	7. seven
wreath	8. eight
wringer	9. nine
wren	10. ten

"b" is silent

"t" is silent

lamb	whistle
thumb	castle
dumb	wrestle
numb	bustle
crumbs	rustle
bomb	rustling
bomber	whistling
comb	wrestling
climb	listen
climber	glisten
climbing	often
	soften

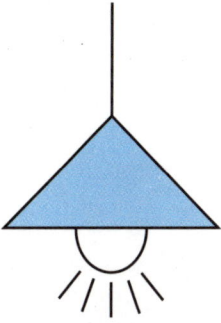

igh = i—e

light
bright
right
night
fight
might
sight
tight

11. eleven
12. twelve
13. thirteen
14. fourteen
15. fifteen
16. sixteen
17. seventeen
18. eighteen
19. nineteen
20. twenty

sigh
high
height

screw

new	30. thirty
flew	40. forty
dew	50. fifty
blew	60. sixty
knew	70. seventy
stew	80. eighty
crew	90. ninety
chew	100. hundred
drew	1000. thousand
mew	
grew	

There, are seven days in a week:
Sunday, Monday, Tuesday, Wednesday.
Thursday, Friday, Saturday.

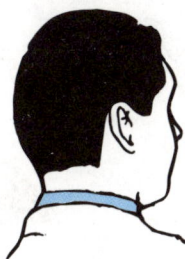 

head	bull
lead	pull
dead	full
bread	put
read	Judy
in‚stead	music
deaf	bull's eye
earth	pudding
early	cushion
leather	butcher
feather	push
weather	bush
	pussy
death	puss
breath	Union Jack

2 = a pair. 6 = half-a-dozen. 12 = a dozen. 20 = a score.

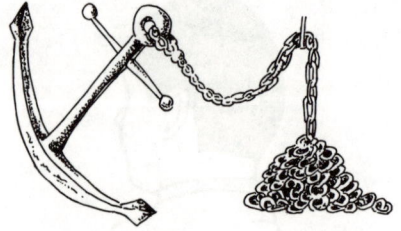

saucer	anchor
Paul	school
Maud	chemist
cause	chorus
be,cause	echo
fault	Christ
daughter	Christmas
sauce	orchestra
sausages	ear-ache
Santa Claus	tooth-ache
	head-ache

"C" is soft

pencil	cill
cigar	cinders
cigarette	cinema
city	

oo, ou, ow , wa, all, ng,

oa, ow , ce, aw, au , ge,

kn, wr, mb, igh, oo, ew ,

sh, th, ch, wh, qu, ce, ge,

ou, ow , all, ay, ai ,

wa, oa, ow , ee, ea ,

a—e, o—e, u—e, i—e, e—e,

aw, au , wr, kn, igh, mb.

The Months:
January, February, March, April, May, June, July, August, September, October, November, December.

43

elephant	station
nephew	nation
telephone	motion
gramophone	notion
Philip	lotion
photo	dic,ta,tion
photograph	sub,trac,tion
Phyllis	add,i,tion
physic	exam,in,a,tion

Revision

chapter, ashes, smith, whist, spelling, escape, divide, even, flute, before, cry, air, airways, fairy, daytime, away, needle, dream, beside, behind, equal, quiz, quarry, smooth, powder, cloudy, mountain, wash, want, ball, shawl, coast, low, below, dance, ambulance, gentleman, badge, know, knew, wrong, crumb, light, heather, healthy, put, because, caught, head-ache, pencil, station.

Memory Words

one, once: Mr., Mrs.: they:
any, many, again, says, said:
mother, other, brother, cover,
money, love, glove, above,
come, some, honey, money,
front, colour, sponge, won,
month, wonder, among,
tongue, son, country, couple,
touch, blood, flood, cousin:
friend: aunt: do, to, too, two,
you, your, shoes: walk, talk,
chalk:

roll, roller, motor: pilot, pirate, library, silent, silence, sign, giant: thief, chief, field, fierce, believe: navy, gravy, lady, baby: pony: tiny: tough, rough, enough, laugh, cough: would, could, should: fruit, suit, juice: live, give, build, building, built: policeman, scissors: sword: worm, word, work, worker, world: old, bold, soldier: door, floor: ceiling: hour, ghost, shepherd: through.

HINTS FOR SECOND INFANT YEAR

Having established a firm phonic basis in Book 1 we now introduce gradually the *names* of letters. See pages 4 to 10 where vowel changes are presented.

As the weeks go by, tackle the consonants thus:

     "b" (sound) spells b (name)
     "c" (sound) spells c (name)

until you have completed the alphabet.

Impress on the children that if while reading they meet a new word, they will sound it as usual. If that fails, the teacher will help. By the end of the school year children will be able to spell their own name and short simple words.

NOTE FOR NON ENGLISH-SPEAKING PUPILS

1 . Where there is difficulty with the sound of 'th', an easy solution is to provide a small mirror, ask the child to put out his/her tongue then say "this", "that", etc. The following week practise words *ending* with 'th'.

2. The sound made by 'wh'. Ignore the English habit of dropping the letter 'h'. Proceed as shown on page 47 of Book 1.

An activity book entitled *Sound and Write — Book 2* is also available to reinforce the phonic skills taught in this book.